salmonpoetry

Publishing Irish & International Poetry Since 1981

Published in 2018 by
Salmon Poetry
Cliffs of Moher, County Clare, Ireland
Website: www.salmonpoetry.com
Email: info@salmonpoetry.com

Copyright © Thomas Kabdebo, 2018

ISBN 978-1-910669-84-7

All rights reserved. No part of this publication may be reproduced or transmitted in any form or by any means, electronic or mechanical, including photography, recording, or any information storage or retrieval system, without permission in writing from the publisher. The book is sold subject to the condition that it shall not, by way of trade or otherwise, be lent, resold or otherwise circulated without the publisher's prior consent in any form of binding or cover other than that in which it is published and without a similar condition, including this condition, being imposed on the subsequent purchaser.

COVER IMAGE: *Dreamstime*
COVER DESIGN & TYPESETTING: *Siobhán Hutson*

Printed in Ireland by Sprint Print

*Salmon Poetry gratefully acknowledges the support of
The Arts Council / An Chomhairle Ealaoín*

*To Daina and
to my mother's memory*

Acknowledgements

Acknowledgement is due to the editors of the following publications in which a number of these poems, or versions of them, have appeared: *Penultima hora, Az Istenek,* and *Fortified Princeccriptions.*

Contents

Homer and Odysseus	11
From Guyana	12
Attila József	13
Raindrop and Candleflame	14
Hungary in 1957	15
Personal Departure	16
Roary Lyon	17
Jutka	18
On a postage stamp with very small letters	19
Live as if	20
To the smiling sun	21
Questions	22
Stretched by Your Hand	23
Our elders ...	24
Awakening	25
Christ	27
Outwitting Question	28
Dublin and Maynooth Haikus	29
Three piece suit	30
Roma	31
The football fan	32
Journey around my heart	33
Raft	35
The Bionic Boy, Isti	36
The book of life and death	37
Nausikaa, who was she?	38
Böbe and Danubius	39
Adwise	40
Jesus and Einstein	41
Francesco, the pope	42
About the author	46

Ultima Ora

Homer and Odysseus

Homer sat on a stone
on the seashore
Odysseus was about
gathering baits for him.

From Guyana

I'm facing the dawn: here, between the shutters, one has to stare the new sun in the eye. Cows amble on the snake-infested pasture; in the ditch fish move, the size of a fist. Mildew is spreading on the walls of the houses. Mildew flourishes like lilies among the sedges, like viper-tails at the feet of sugar canes. Like the earth that seemingly sets out as if all the kernels of dust would come to life. In front of you, behind you, on both sides, there are endless columns of ants. It took a generation before the sling sped you across the ocean as if you were mere stone. Europe was congested ; Albion pale and dank. Your birthplace nothing but a gopher hole. And now, in this 100 degree heat, you may ponder, soaked in sweat, the key to tropical lifestyle. Actually why are you in Guyana? Was it pre-destined? Are you a blacksmith? Is Iron your fate? Or are you made of Iron? Ever question palm trees conscious at the edge of the horizon? Do they know why they give birth to coconuts the size of jugs? Do the idle alligators of the swamps know how to survive when the dry season swoops down? Does the ocean sense why it spits out logs, casts out reeking whales, teeming, starved crabs? They'd love to crawl back into the ocean as infant turtles do but they are marooned on the beach. Only one reaches home out of a thousand! Why is reflected on my tanned skin. Daybreak, scarlet sky. EIDENAL—my craving is called EIDENAL—stimulates me. My eyes are bewitched by the glorious sun. Pain leaves like a cloud whipped by wind—the first bat of dawn. How the swallows race back and forth! Let my magnolia tree teem with thrush. Let the fish-hawk draw it's circles. Let the ember-colored (sic) ibis set off for the North. I want the sun slowly to pour its white gold on the streaming landscape.

(Translated by Nicholas Kolumban)

Attila József

I knew
your wife,
nephew
and sister.
You were
the greatest
poet
but otherwise
a blister.

Raindrop and Candleflame

THIS IS A DEADLY A DEADLY HIS
THIS IS A DEADLY A DEADLY HIS

S

S

KIY

THIS IS A DEADLY A DEADLY A DEADLY
THIS IS A DEADLY A DEADLY

Hungary in 1957

Don't be sad:
this will not last forever;
did we turn Turkish
in 150 years? We did
never, never, never.

Personal Departure

The deed is done
I'm gone
this was not fun.
You could have come.
It is sad when a
dad
absenting his daughters
Lily and Panda
and decides to
run.

Roary Lyon

There was rage in my heart and fury
frustration,
gargoyles came, devils, no sleep.
In the tempest of my outrage
the sinew-ropes of my body heaved
and that "fragile barca". the soul
was close to shipwreck.
Then your letter came
and I saw
—in the tiny mirror-receptacles of my mind—
I saw your eyes
Their deep velvet came into focus.
Caresses lay in it, like lazy pussycats.
And the king of these cats
jumped on the tip of my pen:
"General Roary Lyon, I am!"

Jutka

because Lollobrigida
is not in town.

On a postage stamp with very small letters

The wind is asleep on the wings of a wasp
you overstretched yourself
nothing is in your grasp.
Reached out for everything
and held hardly anything
you lived through better
and cannot hope for worse.
All things are now amiss
and you are a final kiss
on the bottom of your universe.

Live as if

Live as if the world would be
snapped up by the sun
in the next minute.
    —Don't,
    for your cells will transmit only
    breathless desperation.
Thrust with the whole of the self
be the arrow
the flame
the lion's teeth
the serpent's tongue.
    —And of your own jolting, perish?
    Does the oil that burns
    justify the killing of the whale?
Not another thought to it.
Cut with the sword!
Through Gordion knots,
off Gorgon's head …
    —Wait. Do what you must.
    But pause
    and pray for his and your own soul
    —as at Holy Communion—
    before you pounce upon the prey.

To the smiling sun

when you regain your touch with the things around you
and come to terms with the things within:
start again to invest your care in those without.
It is like rising after the fall.
Still feel the pain but it does not hurt any more
and the healing rays of the sun pour into your pores
and you undertake the chores without a shrug.
More than that: with a smile.
And while it lasts you hope it will last forever,
and feeling as you do, both good and strong
you undertake to mould the days that lie ahead
and to shape the hours of the future
with the gymnast's care of the mind,
who stands at the foot of a giant swing
and knows he will ride through the ups and downs
batting his eyelids only once
when he gets near the smiling sun.

Questions

Do you know the feeling
when things like lost books stray birds and people
reappear and find their place again?

When moments join like hands
and minutes wed
and hours and days are born with meaning,

when holes have their fill
and prey beasts do not kill
and a cause has his sister reason,

when you count like a bead on the abacus
counting and counted
with recurring patience,
then the colours merge
and the landscapes lulls and the waves of the river
beat within your pulse,

and with crowns linked up
and roots as veins interwoven
you live like a tree conscious of the woods?

Stretched by Your Hand

Your bonnet nearly caught the flame
of your blonde coloured hair,
your feet made the stones delirious
when you, heronlike stepped on them
and with joy the tiny pearl was bouncing,
for it touched your snowhite neck
and the old wood dreamt of his youth
when, like a stork, you nested in the chair …
… and a button I would like to be
   or just an elastic band
dwelling on your pants and petticoats:
caressed, touched or stretched by your hand.

Our elders　　　　　　　wrote abo
ut humming bees　　　and wilting flowe
rs and a heart that felt　　the agony of moods. W
e look about and humming　aeroplanes and roving roc
kets synchronise our illusions　with visions that outnumber
beings and bees. The flowers turn plastic and the heart jum
ps out of its onomastic cage and is planted like flowers of o
ld. An equivocal age when the gardeners of the heart let it bl
ossom in different bosoms, yet cannot cut out the rage with t
he damaged stems of veins and arteries. From two-hearted
refugees and wandering Jews to wandering hearts from ch
est to chest we accept the symbol of suffering with one of
our hearts while the other forces us to conform to the fo
rm of the crocodile's heart placed on our cards. The pl
ayers are mortal but the game is immortal. When los
ing, our morals are shifting and our morale is drift
ing below the degree of lowest expectations. Wh
en winning we cash in minutes from the unacc
ountable sum of infinity. Old cores are corro
ded and new ones are coded, yet everythi
ng is goaded in to one heart: the beats
of all hearts, the surge of the blood
of all surgeons, poems rotating
in the pulse and a word with
out rival: survival surviv
al survival survival su
rvival survival sur
vival survival s
urvival surv
ival surviv
al survi
val sur
vival

Awakening

It was asleep, hibernating, counting its atoms
but still it was a living bud,
it needed only a sign,
a ray of light, to cause it to break into flower....

(it extended to the consciousness
call it resurrection,
it multiplied and centred on a goal
call it parousia)

In the twilight world between sleep and awakening,
fever and recovery, questions flashed on the inner screen
of what was once and what will be on the mind:
if you can journey to the stars,
if beings from yonder could reach to you,
why couldn't I reach beyond the stars?
if the DNA carries the plan of the psychological build-up,
won't my actions hold the key to my own future makeup?
if the mammoth flesh could last in ice, the grains in pyramids,
shouldn't my cells have been planned for a new awakening?
if ESP can operate and faith-healing recuperate the broken mind,
if cosmic rays can penetrate and particles can play havoc
with what it-is-and-was-will-be, casuality-fatality,
why couldn't there be immortality?

... it was a journey that permitted
not just a change of place
but a change of sphere in the universe...

—not a place but a sphere it was
which answered the primitive in us:
"cobs of green corn were never lacking
pumpkins and grass and green pepper
and there were the gods known as Tlaloques living
like the priests of the idols with long hair".

Christ

As Tom saw him sometimes: He was a hobo with a dozen layabouts
on the road, day and night, begging, talking, walking;
the sun beat down, their sweat mingled with the smell
of olives and distant orchids.
His hands forgot the plane, smoothened out,
but the feet roughened in the sandals
so when the shadows went to sleep he often couldn't,
and kept on pestering the stones and the stars.

He knew no woman, was very fond of kids
and always talked to them about his Dad;
some say, he was a good fellow, too good really,
others, that he was mad.

And as he sees Tom: There you are, the cleverest of them all—
so you believe, the only thing you do believe
but I don't.
Touch me! And push your thumb in hard,
as you would push—in stretch of time—
the button of a machine-gun.
Words of doubt are bullets in my ribs,
yet each time I break, (the strongest when weakest
like all of you) I win:
you get convinced.
Not sweat not thorns not even the piercing lance
did hurt as much as a single faithless glance
that killed me.
But I rose again. Since before the doubt existed
I am.

Winner of the New York International Prize in 1971. Now dedicated to Pope Francis.

Outwitting Question

If a Greek can outwit
ten neophites
how many fools
can be trapped by
an Armenian?

Dublin and Maynooth Haikus

The rain stopped mid air
I missed a heart-beat
She ran to me on the street.

(Maynooth Seasons) Image in the pond
Swallows are building their nests
broken by the rain.

Coming up for air
Goldfish spy birds spying on them
surface impressions.

Caterpillar's boat
red leaf from a silver birch
food for fishy thought.

Wafer-thin the ice
a bird's beak pickaxed it
my pond's broken bond.

Three piece suit

1. Train your shadow

You must train your shadow
to rest while you run
and walk away when you sit down.
How else to survive?
(with someone always dogging your heels?)

2. A gentle warning

Two knives made love
blunting one another.
two saws made love
their teeth fall out,
when I carve soft bread.

3. Fragment

Under the limitless sky
she sat down and cried:
"the meadows, the buildings, the people…"
—meadows by buildings,
—buildings by people,
"… and even the people the people are occupied".

Roma

When I reached St. Peter's Square
my knees were no longer square
I was humming Roma, Roma
like a watch that goes again
like a watch that goes again.

The football fan

Two rattles and a whistle
three bundles of toilet roll
ready to throw at the keeper
when he lets in the first goal;
windswept cheeks and feverish eyes
voice croakin' of boos and cheers
shaking fists and locks and tufts
pristine joys and primitive fears:
a pintsize mans who would commune
with crowd and players alike
mingle sensations and senses unite
for moments of hits and missus
when his team leads he offers his fags
at the spot kick he lifts his lame left leg.

A poisoned arrow was shot in his knee,
holding a stick, now he is referee;
at the edge of the bush, women
chant and jungle their beads,
the team of the Gahuku leads—
men must staple the Gama eleven
A missionary taught them the game
scores of years before,
now it's transfused in a rite
by him who became a medicine man.
For days on end they kick the ball
until the sides equal the score.

Journey around my heart

My chest is stuffed with pain. Angina pectoris,
atria, ventricles, a flame-red piece of flesh,
telegraph-wire veins, cable-like arteries,
braids of coronaries crowing the happy bride,
(funeral wreaths on the coffin of the deceased)?
A pretty wench whispers softly: 'How I loved you".
You're silting up by slow degrees, stealthily,
the sediments are damming up your arteries,
you blood's a throbbing goblin, your heart heaves space,
reaching beneath your breastbone nightmares squeeze you tight.
One must be brave. Your heartbeat galloping away
at a hundred and seven, you are dead-beat with fright.
The Reaper frightens you? That he may gash a vein
and you may end up sailing a Red Sea of your own?
Calm down. You need a rest. Sleep soundly through the night,
have dreams, re-dream your lathery season of youth.
canoeing down the Danube from Ulm to Baja,
and scaling the summit of Mount Roraima
re-dream your steady heartbeat which broke into a sprint
when you caught sight of Kati running ball.
You wake. Today there will be no ball games at all.
You hear your sweetheart softly breathing. Lusting swells:
you share a double bed for sleep ... and something else.
Go, reach for her! Your heart purrs in you, aroused;
from purring arousal on to savage carousal,
blood races in the veins: halt! it-is-not-al-lowed.
Road blocks obstruct the way. DEAD SLOW commands a sign.
Shoals of squid stare at you as you lie half asleep,
see the crimson coloured crustaceans of the deep,
the bright distemper lighting up an ancient picture ...
which one has stained the patient's chest? You may conjecture.

Catheter crawls towards the heart in slow meanders,
the healing Aesculapean serpent? One wonders.
Doctors spotlessly white. Some X-ray photographs.
Constricted coronaries. Open the bloodgates!
Who needs a sluice when the dams are breached? We slumber.
The Danube and I. They hatched me into halves.
My femoral vein will be used for updates.
(Many streams drip feed us and brooks without number).

Translated by Peter Zollman

Raft

We travelled down on a raft which was like a swimming forest: the trees lying on their belly, flattened out overf the fast, narrow river, all huddled together and holding on to one another with iron claws.

My father was balancing in the middle, and I beside him translating each tremor of the waves, each kick from a stone trembles of fear and delight.

Two woodcutters, a Ruthenian and a Rumanian shared the helm, and at the front a Slovak stood smiling and pushed and shoved off the cliffs, boulders and stones with a boat-hook.

Suddenly, the hook got stuck in the cleft of a cliff and the Slovak, holding on steadfast to the pole was hurtled in front of us.

—My father turned white

There's no stopping downwards a mountain.

No depth to a mountain-river.

No force to stop a rolling forest.

The cut-down-trees crackled; the broken surface had no time to heal.

The woodcutters lowered their eyes.

—But I, the ignorant child, turned back and looked. and their behind us, a head emerged from the water, two hands gripping the top pf the boulder and a huge grin of fright and joy stamped on his face:
the Slovak.

The Bionic Boy, Isti

He wanted to fly like Icarus
from the top of our whitebeam tree
(I rushed to him like Dedalus)
bruised, battered by branches and twigs
crash-landed with broken limbs did he.

His right wrist fractured in a triangle
(we were under a monstrous spell)
he stretched out and whined like a little pup
Were you asleep guardian angel, were you there?
He was! His head in my palm as he fell."

While waiting for the ambulance
I ran through my falls in a trance:
a tumble from a horse in front of a train,
a jump under a floating raft,
and the bullet that missed me in France.

Now back from the clinic, the bionic boy,
up to his armpits in plaster cast,
paints with his mouth, and plays the keyboard
of the family P.C. with all his toes,
then winks. The future winks the past.

The book of life and death

I've tried to picture the records of *karma* and *dharma* in computer terms, in vain. Networks are nonplussed, computers crash, their entrails are consumed by viruses. One thunderstorm and databases lose all their memories. The records of life and death are written in a gigantic book, magnificently illustrated by the pictures of every animal and plant *who* had ever lived. The book is bound in the hinds of tyrants: not just the napoleons'—hitlers'—stalins'—idiamins'—saddamhusseins' skin, but those of school bullies too. Huge as it is, the book keeps on growing, the pages are already taller than the topmost cloud over the Himalayas, AND WIDER THAN THE GAP BETWEEN ARABS AND JEWS. The leaves of the book are made of special parchment, the skins of unborn babies in this world. The story of one calendar year fills one single leaf, in six columns, each year to a given page. The writing, on either side of the leaf, is either in black ink—showing the chronicles of the living—or in invisible ink, recording but not yet revealing their present. (There are some red pages in the book written in martyr-blood.)

You cannot hope to read even one chapter of the Book of Life and Death, because each chapter is longer than a lifetime, the runic columns are too dense with hieroglyphic letters, the margins are covered with cross-references, and below there are umpteen footnotes. But you may browse in it if you were talented in deciphering puzzles, finding exits to mazes, and solving conundrums. For reading you need a periscopic telescope, because in the sea of real and potential sicknesses, where your life-craft floats, half-submerged, the seaweed of your tangles troubles blur clear vision. Smudged, with the edges curiously frayed, there is a foxed page, no. 1998, with a direct reference to you. Not your eventual fate—it is still in invisible ink—nor your genealogy, this takes up a few cross-references elsewhere, but your stamp on the world, your real significance.

Well you are a footnote to a footnote to the stream of dreams wafting around the vapours of the Danube.

Nausikaa, who was she?

A dragonfly—
a moll—a woman
not a guy,
my butterfly!

Böbe and Danubius

According to our president
my efforts were
very well spent.
Anyway, and anyhow
Danubius is top book now,
and as for
Ament, she
keeps my love:
Amen.

Adwise

Remember P. Kati!
It is better to give
than to receive

Jesus and Einstein

The miracle is solved by Einstein
Jesus came through the bolted door
then he bodily walked on the floor
"Come on Thomas, touch me with your finger
Some of you believe without a touch."

Francesco, the pope

To Pope (not to Dryden's friend)
"this poetry will never cease,
this will go through
war and peace"

Omega and Alpha
Sicitur ad Alpha
did not wish that Helena
should my wife be:
Helenka

In 2017, THOMAS KABDEBO was nominated by the Hungarian Prime Minister as Hungary's poet laureate.